Made in the USA
Columbia, SC
03 May 2022

59891287R00057